JOEN WOLFROM

VISUAL

COLORING

A FOOLPROOF APPROACH TO COLOR-RICH QUILTS

Lora,
Happy coloring !
Joen Wolfrom :)

C&T PUBLISHING

Text © 2007 Joen Wolfrom

Artwork © 2007 C&T Publishing, Inc., and Joen Wolfrom

Publisher: *Amy Marson*

Editorial Director: *Gailen Runge*

Acquisitions Editor: *Jan Grigsby*

Editor: *Liz Aneloski*

Technical Editors: *Wendy Mathson* and *Gayle Gallagher*

Technical Writer: *Darra Williamson*

Copyeditor/Proofreader: *Wordfirm Inc.*

Cover Designer: *Christina Jarumay*

Design Director/Book Designer: *Rose Sheifer-Wright*

Illustrator: *Wendy Mathson*

Production Coordinator: *Zinnia Heinzmann*

Nature Photography © 2007 Joen Wolfrom and Lonnie Brock (when noted)

Quilt Photography by Ken Wagner (unless otherwise noted)

Published by C&T Publishing, Inc., P.O. Box 1456, Lafayette, CA 94549

Front cover: *North Wind*, Lois E. Dunten and *Ebb and Flow*, Adrienne Lindsay Cannon

Library of Congress Cataloging-in-Publication Data

Wolfrom, Joen.
  Visual coloring : a foolproof approach to color-rich quilts / Joen Wolfrom.
     p. cm.
  Includes bibliographical references and index.
  ISBN-13: 978-1-57120-398-4 (paper trade : alk. paper)
  ISBN-10: 1-57120-398-2 (paper trade : alk. paper)
  1. Patchwork--Patterns. 2. Quilting--Patterns. 3. Color in art. I. Title.

  TT835.W64425 2006
  746.46--dc22

                    2006029243

Printed in China
10 9 8 7 6 5 4

Contents

Dedication

This book is dedicated to my family, who has graciously and lovingly supported my passions, my whims, my travels, and my extraordinary deadlines throughout these many years. So with love, I give many thanks to those who are most important in my life: Dan, Danielle, Dane, David, Mike, Cheri, Jack, Joseph, and Micah.

Acknowledgments

I thank all who have played a role in the creation of *Visual Coloring*. This book's strength is in the contributions and talents of many people to whom I am indebted. My ideas for this book could never have come to fruition if it were not for the help, goodwill, talent, and support of many. Thank you so very much!

First, I wish to acknowledge Darra Williamson's role in bringing the seed of this idea into book form. Several years ago, we spent the weekend brainstorming and visualizing how this book could evolve. We had a lovely, creative time, and both of us are ecstatic that this book is a reality. Also, I thank Darra for lightening my load by offering her technical writing talents; she wrote the instructions for the projects. Thank you, Darra!

I wish to thank each quilter who accepted the challenge to create a quilt by using visual coloring to select colors and fabrics. Their quilts amaze me—they far surpassed my expectations. What an unbelievable group of quilters they are!

I thank Mickie Swall for the long hours she put in and for her excellent workmanship. Many thanks to Lois Dunten and Patsy Preiss, who did more than their share of burning the midnight oil. Also, I thank Joanne Williams for her beautiful finishing handwork! (I couldn't do it without her!)

Gayla Burger, Karen Dovala, Kelly Edwards, Pat Harrison, Veronica Nurmi, and Mickie Swall beautifully machine quilted all the instructional and project quilts. Their quilting talents and workmanship are second to none. Thank you for being so flexible!

This unusual book relied heavily on my nature photography. Thanks must be given to Freeman Patterson, Lonnie Brock, and André Gallant, whose professional photographic knowledge and creative talents have not only helped me to improve my photography skills but also have inspired and encouraged me to broaden my imagination. I still have much to learn, but almost everything I know is a result of their instructional skills, creative minds, and patience. In addition, I wish to thank Lonnie Brock for sharing a selection of his nature photography. I am honored to include his work!

A grateful thanks goes to my editor, Liz Aneloski. As the editor of my last five books, Liz understands my writing goals, appreciates my challenges, accepts my quirks, and supports my creative streak. I love her!

Joen

Visual Coloring

Can I make beautiful quilts without knowing any color theory?

YES

Is there a fun, fast, easy way to select colors for my quilts?

YES

Is there a way to pick my quilts' colors without being surprised at the end?

YES

The easiest way to select colors for your quilts is with a method I call visual coloring. It is fun and easy. It gives great results—and perhaps best of all—it takes very little time to learn.

Join me in this wonderful adventure to unlock the keys to selecting colors and fabrics for your quilts. There's no risk, no anguish, and no pain. Instead, the time you spend choosing colors and fabrics will be filled with exciting realizations and fun exploration. Visual coloring is a simple step to color independence and—it could be the most important journey in your creative life!

Joen

I love color! I especially love beautifully colored quilts—quilts that are stunningly dramatic, visually exciting, richly autumnal, quietly subdued, and refreshingly cool. I find beauty in both quiet hues and brilliant colors. I have rarely met a color I didn't like! You may be like I am, or you may be more discerning about your color preferences.

The big question for quilters isn't what colors do we like, but how can we use the colors we love to create the beautiful quilts we envision? I pondered this question many years ago, which led me to devise a simple color-selection method. I have named this method visual coloring.

Visual coloring allows us to work with colors successfully in an almost foolproof manner. It trains our eyes to see the subtle nuances in nature's colors. The colors and fabrics incorporated in every quilt in this book were selected by using visual coloring. Before immersing ourselves in the idea of visual coloring, let's look at some of the most important aspects of our relationship with color.

Color Influences

No matter how old you are or how long you have been quilting, it's important that you get in tune with the colors you intuitively respond to in a positive way. Each of us responds to colors and color combinations positively or negatively, depending on our makeup and life experiences.

Many of our color responses have much to do with where we grew up, where we have spent most of our adult lives, and our life experiences. These influences are often so subtle that we aren't even aware of them. If we think back to our early experiences, we may find clues to many of our color loves and dislikes. It may be interesting to see how environment, geographic region, and culture play a role in the colors we intuitively love. Different regions provide their own unique natural colorings. Our color favorites are deeply rooted in the areas we know best and in those we feel most at home.

If you grew up in or near a desert, you may have a natural affinity for the strong desert hues: the warm earth tones, the strong blue skies, and the brilliant hues of the wildflowers.

If you are from the desert, you know how stunning the textures and colors of rock formations can be, particularly when highlights and shadows accentuate their beauty. No doubt your memory bank is filled with

Ablaze with Color—The desert is in its glory with the vivid colors of the wildflowers. Photo courtesy of Lonnie Brock, nature photographer.

visions of the breathtaking desert hues of the sunrises and sunsets. The blend of earthy cacti colors, set against the desert sky, is second nature to you. It would be difficult to remove the desert colors from your subconscious mind.

Likewise, if you moved to the desert as an adult, or visit it often, then its color characteristics may have subtly become part of your color personality.

The tropical regions are rich in dramatic colors too. The flowers are exquisite in pure colors—the greens so very lush. Even the birds exude a brilliance that is rare in northern regions. I doubt that a person who lives in the natural brilliance of tropical colors could remain unaffected by their exuberance. People who live in these regions may have an affinity to strong, pure-spirited hues.

If you grew up in a land of mountains, evergreen forests, sparkling lakes, fjords, rivers, and other waterways, your love for green and blue hues may be substantial. These preferences could easily include the beautiful water hues that are so dazzling—aqua greens, aqua blues, teals, turquoises, deep blues, emerald greens, blue-violets (periwinkle), lavenders, yellow-greens, chartreuses, and deep olives. No doubt, the blues and soft violets of distant mountains are deep in your memory too.

At sunrise and sunset, you can see the wonderful play of colors in both the sky and the water. Violet, orange, lavender, gold, coral, pink, magenta—all can be seen in both subtle and stunning drama.

The Desert in Its Stunning Beauty—Desert vegetation is like no other. It's filled with magical color inspiration. Photo courtesy of Lonnie Brock, nature photographer.

The Land of Forests and Mountains—The evergreen forests and mountain ranges are filled with green and blue hues, which are featured dramatically in areas such as America's Pacific Northwest.

The vast countryside has its own rich blend of colors, often varying greatly with the season. Fields may be ablaze with brilliant yellows, oranges, chartreuses, or other strong colorings as crops reach maturity. During much of the year, the subtle greens, browns, and rich earth tones are exhibited quietly. These understated colorings become deeply embedded in people who have lived in one of the many farming regions of our country.

In the countryside, the feeling of spaciousness is so apparent. The open land and huge sky seem to form a grand partnership that provides magnificent color combinations awaiting our interpretations.

Fields Shimmer with Vivid Color—The beautiful colors you see in farming regions vary greatly with the seasons and the crops. Here, a field ablaze in the brilliant colors of the rape plant contrasts with the red of the barn and the deep green of the hills in the distance. Photo courtesy of Lonnie Brock, nature photographer.

A Magnificent Partnership—The open fields and rangelands form a great color partnership with the sky. Their palette can be striking or quite mellow. Here, the sky provides wonderful hues to blend with the rich fields. Photo courtesy of Lonnie Brock, nature photographer.

Think about the natural colors of the area where you grew up. How do you respond to these colors? If you are not certain, begin noticing your reactions to colors that are common to the region where you spent the most time in your childhood.

If you moved from region to region as you grew up, your color personality may be more complex and more difficult to discern. Visualize the regions you loved best. What colors come to mind when you think of these regions? Your natural color inclinations may arise either from the region where you lived the longest or from the area where you were the happiest.

Drama at Day's End—Sunsets are filled with glorious colors that can elicit many emotive feelings. Each sunset is like an exquisite palette. It gives us the opportunity to reflect on another beautiful way to put colors together. Take advantage of these color inspirations by recording them with your camera.

THE BLENDING OF CULTURAL AND REGIONAL INFLUENCES

In the United States, we are a compilation of so many countries rich with traditions and cultures. Many regions of our country are microcosms of the cultures of far-off lands.

For example, there is a strong northern European influence in the Pacific Northwest because so many of its early settlers came from the Scandinavian countries, where many geographical features are so similar. This population's naturally reserved personality, combined with the area's natural resources, helps define this region's historical color use. Warm wood tones, neutrals, and the blue hues of sky and water have been the mainstay colors of the Pacific Northwest for generations.

The color use and color spirit of faraway lands, such as Italy, Turkey, South Africa, China, and Japan, are part of our country's color history,

and the cultural and geographic features of these regions meld in our country's colors. Natural geographic influences, the origins of an area's settlers, and the influence of new residents blend together to set a regional color pattern.

Close your eyes and allow your mind to see the colors of your childhood region. Reflect on how these early influences have affected your color choices in both your home and your quilts. Do the same for the area where you currently live. Find and use the colors you are naturally drawn to as much as you can.

THE ART OF SEEING

When I was young, I believed that sky and water were blue, grass was green, sand was tan, stones were gray, tree trunks were brown, and apples were red. You could have asked me the color of almost anything, and I am quite certain that I would have been able to tell it to you in the blink of

an eye. You probably would have given similar responses. As children, we *knew* the color of any item without giving it a second thought.

One evening in my fourth decade of life, I had a color epiphany while observing a glorious sunset. That experience awoke in me the realization that I had never noticed how nature painted the world in colors. I had not really been aware of the colors my eyes saw.

It was a profound awakening for me to realize that *knowing* the colors and *seeing* the colors were two different concepts. I was startled to find that my mind had been working in *color assumption mode* for as long as I could remember. It was then that I decided to seriously train my eyes to really take note of the colors I saw and to stop making color assumptions that relied on color labeling, which is easy but not very accurate.

Soon after this experience, a simple idea for selecting colors for my quilts came to me. I experimented with the idea on quilts. It was easy and fun, and, best of all, it gave me the guidance I needed to select colors and fabrics. Thus was born the idea of **visual coloring**.

Visual coloring works for everyone, regardless of color experience. It doesn't matter whether you are a color theorist extraordinaire or you have never opened a color book. This method provides you with color confidence as you create beautiful quilts.

FIRST STEPS TO VISUAL COLORING

The first step to visual coloring is finding out what colors and color combinations you are drawn to. Your intuitive color attractions are the foundation for visual coloring.

To begin, set a date to have a relaxing day, listening to your favorite music, keeping your favorite beverage close at hand, and looking through magazines, calendars, date books, greeting cards, photos, and other similar material in search of color combinations that you absolutely love. Be certain to keep this date with yourself—it's an important first step in creating beautiful quilts in the colors you love.

As you look through your selections, pull out all images that attract you deeply: those that take your breath away, those filled with unbelievable beauty, those that give you a sense of serenity, and those that bring you excitement or drama. Sort these images into visual groups (you can use file folders to organize the images), such as brightly colored hues; soft, quiet colorings; autumnal colorations; and perhaps wintry hues.

As you find new color-inspiration images you love, add them to your files. Once you begin, you'll find all sorts of color inspiration you will want to duplicate in your quilts. Subconsciously, your eyes will continue to search for the color combinations you love.

Keep these color-inspiration files handy so you can thumb through the images frequently to get your subconscious mind to begin thinking about the colors for your next project. On these facing pages are samplings of color-inspiration images I have placed into different files.

Dramatic Color-Inspiration File—
I have dozens of bold color-inspiration images in this file because I love strong, clear colors. Flowers and sunsets are great for providing dramatic coloring. Not all images need to be from nature. The chartreuse image is a photo of a mixture of water and food coloring.

Quiet Color-Inspiration File—Winter scenes, quiet nature scenes, and grayed colors (tones) can all be part of this file. You can divide it further by color or the emotions the images evoke.

As you begin thinking about a new project, pull out your files and study your images. You will probably find yourself responding to the colors in one image more than any other. Those colors are the ones your creative spirit is most in tune with at that particular time.

You may notice that you respond differently to colors as the seasons come and go and as your mood changes. One image might appeal to you most at one time, and another might tug at your heart later.

If you find yourself responding to two or more images equally, you will have to decide which one to use. Generally, the decision is based on which colors work best with the pattern you have selected or the fabrics you have available.

Serene Color-Inspiration File—I love serene color inspiration. The colors are so clear and striking even though they are reflective in nature. Here are a few photos from my file.

SELECTING COLORS AND FABRICS WITH VISUAL COLORING

When using visual coloring, you are actually selecting your colors and fabrics simultaneously. Quite simply, you are choosing fabrics to use that visually *read* like the colors in the image. You are matching fabric colors with the image colors. After you have selected your image, I recommend that you enlarge it to fit on an 8½″ × 11″ sheet of paper (or other similar size). Enlarging the image allows you to see the colors more easily than if you were working with a small image. Unexpected colors are more readily seen in enlarged images.

I have included two visual coloring examples to illustrate the concept of pulling colors from the color-inspiration image and fabrics from your stash. These two examples are Falling for Fall and Dance, Iris, Dance.

Falling for Fall

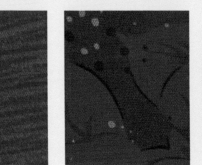

Sample 1: Falling for Fall

I was surprised to find that I kept coming back to this simple photo for color inspiration. When I began choosing the fabrics, I started with the colors my eyes saw first: the rusts, the most brilliant reddish-oranges, and the background greens.

As my eyes became acclimated to the image, I began seeing the soft yellow, apricot, pink, and rose. Notice how closely the fabrics match the photo. Visual coloring is simple to do, and it's a quick way to select both colors and fabrics for your quilts.

This combination of fabrics seems to call for a traditional design, so I'll be designing a traditional-style quilt from this visual coloring image.

Dance, Iris, Dance

Sample 2: Dance, Iris, Dance

This image presents a strong emotive feeling with irises in dramatic colorings. I began choosing fabrics from the most pronounced iris colors first. As I worked, my eyes began seeing many more hues. These unexpected colors can be very important additions, bringing depth or richness to the overall color plan.

I absolutely love the fabrics I chose from this visual coloring, and I am eager to begin designing a quilt with them. These fabrics exude a contemporary feeling for me. Therefore, my design thoughts lean toward an impressionistic garden or a contemporary design.

If more fabrics were needed to create my quilt design, I would head for my local quilt store with my image in hand. In the store, choosing the fabrics that match the colors in my selected image would take only a few minutes.

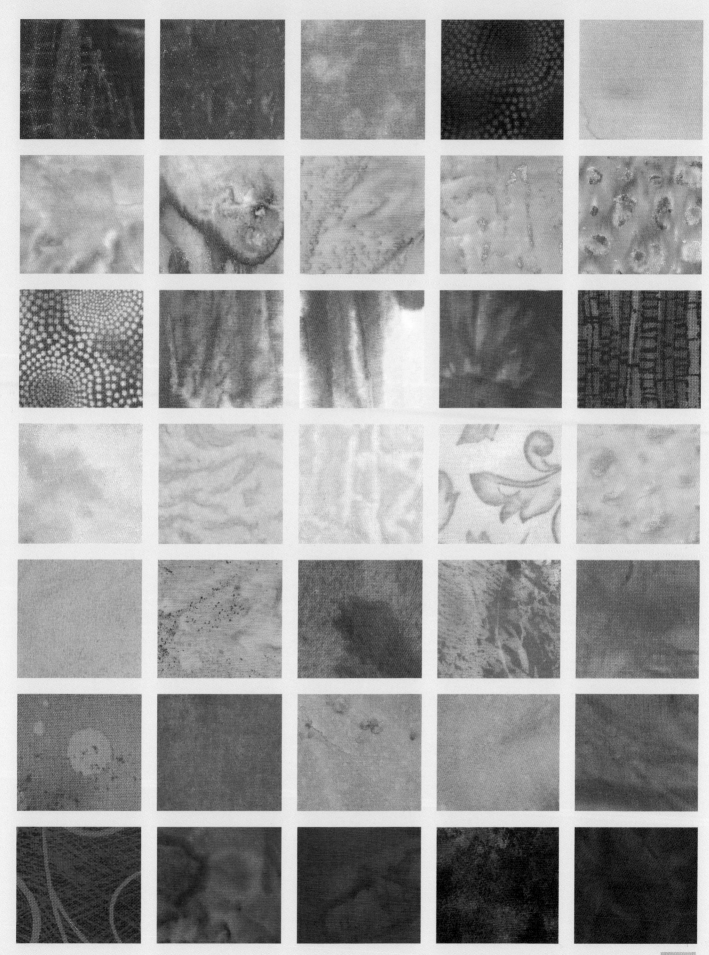

VISUAL COLORING OPTIONS

If you love all the colors in your selected image, and if your design can accommodate it, use all the colors in your quilt. Then your quilt will give you the same feeling as the color image. Unexpected colors often accentuate the overall beauty by adding a rich, unanticipated quality. These hues can cause visual vibration, which gives great excitement or drama to a design. Most often, the surprise colorations in an image are given the role of accent colors. You can give them a larger role if you want to make a more vivid design statement.

Visual coloring is not meant to be rigid. Options may present themselves, giving you slightly different visual paths to consider. Some of the most obvious options are discussed below.

Sharpening Your Color Selection

If you think one color may be too strong, too intense, too light, too dark, or too distracting, eliminate it from your quilt project. For instance, I love the Sunrise in the Rockies image, but I felt that the dark hues of the rocks and grasses were too strong for my quilt's design. I chose to use only the water colors.

Some of the colors in Canadian Sunrise felt too strong for the design I wanted to use, so I omitted the stronger colors here too.

COLOR INSPIRATION:
Sunrise in the Rockies

Sunrise Lattice Stars

COLOR INSPIRATION:
Canadian Sunrise

Misty Morn at Sunrise

You may want to focus only on the foreground colors or on the colors of the main focal point of the picture, choosing to ignore the background colors. For instance, I absolutely love the autumn colors in Impressions of Autumn. However, I felt that the soft blue of the background sky would be distracting, even though it was not very noticeable in the image. I eliminated the sky hues from my quilt.

Lois Dunten and Mary Sorensen made the same decision for their autumnal quilts from the same color-inspiration image (pages 50 and 51).

There are numerous reasons to omit one or more colors from your selected color-inspiration image. If you don't like a color, omit it. If you can't find fabrics to match certain colors, leave them out. If your design can't accommodate all of the colors, you may have to eliminate a few or combine them within certain fabric placements.

Color Proportion

More often than not, you will choose to keep the colors in your quilt in approximately the same proportions as in your color-inspiration image. However, you can change the proportions. You may decide to give another color the lead role. If you change the color proportions, the resulting quilt may elicit quite a different effect than the original imagery, but the quilt will appear related.

An example of changed color proportions is *Star Bright, Snow White*, which uses far more white in its design than the original photo shows.

COLOR INSPIRATION:
Impressions of Autumn

Autumn Log Cabin

COLOR INSPIRATION:
The Sky's the Limit

Star Bright, Snow White

Hybrid Lily (inspired by the colors in Waltz of the Bleeding Heart) and *Pandora's Box* (inspired by Hanging On) used much more plum than the small amount in their respective color-inspiration images.

COLOR INSPIRATION:

Waltz of the Bleeding Heart

Hybrid Lily

COLOR INSPIRATION:

Hanging On

Pandora's Box

Changing or Expanding Values

If you love the colors in your image but want to use lighter hues, do so. Feel free to expand your options by including lighter versions of the colors in your image. For instance, if you are working with orange, you may want to add a soft apricot. If you are working with blue, you may want to include a light blue. Patrice Creswell expanded the values in her quilts *Made in the Shade* and *Fire Bowls*.

If you want to add darker hues in your quilt, consider including darkened versions of the colors in your image. Again, if you are working with orange, you may use a darker version, which might be rust or brown. If you are working with blue, consider adding a darker version of that blue, such as dark blue or navy blue.

Toning Down Your Quilt

If you wish to calm down one or more colors, do so. Simply use fabrics in colors that appear grayer than the colors in the image. The more grayed the colors, the more subdued the results. As hues become grayer, they appear to recede into the design. Instead of using a clear blue, you might add a dusty blue from the same color family. Perhaps you could use a salmon or a grayed apricot instead of a bright orange. *Pieceful Garden* (page 51) is an example of this option, as more toned fabrics are in its background than its color-inspiration image exhibits.

Increasing the Vibrancy of a Color

If you want to create more vibrant coloring than your image shows, add a purer form of the color to your design. If the original color has more gray than you wish, select a fabric that is clearer or appears less grayed. If you want to change a dark blue, select a fabric that is brighter and more pure. If you want to change an apricot, find a fabric closer to pure orange. Keep the color in the same family, just make it closer to its pure form. For example, *Graciela* (page 59) is made using fabrics that are brighter and more pure than its wintry color-inspired hydrangea image.

Fire Bowls

Made in the Shade

Using Other Colorful Inspirations

Nature is not the only place to find color inspiration for visual coloring. You may find beautiful colors that inspire you in pottery, china, wall art, jewelry, a scarf, or some other object that delights you with its colors, vivid or subtle. If you absolutely love the colors of an object, and you want to make a quilt with those colors, use the object to pull the colors and fabrics, as you would a photo.

VISUAL COLORING IN ACTION

In the next few pages you will see examples of visual coloring in action. The color-inspiration image, a selection of fabrics used, and the resulting quilt are shown. You will see a definite color relationship between the image and the quilt.

COLOR INSPIRATION: *Forest Reflecting in the River*

Sample 3: Reflecting Forest

I love the colors in the river scene Forest Reflecting in the River. The reflection of the brilliant greens of the forest in the rushing river seems almost magical. The blue-violet rocks and water sprays are equally enticing. Certainly, many more fabrics could have been used than were chosen.

Generally, as I bring together fabrics, my mind begins playing with design options. I may write ideas down on a piece of paper to play with later. As time allows, I will make rough drawings with a lead pencil, colored pencils, watercolor pencils, or a combination of these tools. I may use an illustrator program on my computer, if that suits my mood. Sometimes I see the project clearly in my mind, so I just go with my vision. Regardless of how I work through my design, eventually the design and colors meld.

For this project, I wanted to use a traditional pattern that would offer multiple design layers and flexibility. I chose King David's Crown— one of my nostalgic block favorites. *Reflecting Forest* is the quilt inspired by the beautiful rushing river.

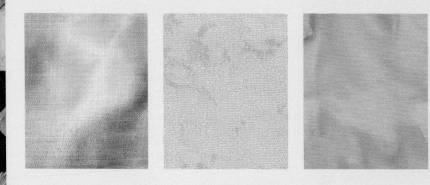

Reflecting Forest, 30″ × 30″, designed by Joen Wolfrom, pieced and quilted by Mickie Swall.

COLOR INSPIRATION: *Canadian Sunrise*

Sample 4: Misty Morn at Sunrise

The soft, gentle colors in this beautiful early morning Canadian sunrise compelled me to take this photo. Feeling that the dark foreground colors were too strong, I decided not to use them in my quilt.

As I chose fabrics using the colors in the photo, I found I had an ample selection for the misty water hues. However, I could find only one fabric that represented the unusual background woodland hues. Because I had only a half-yard of this fabric, my design options were limited.

I felt that this visual coloring required a simple design. The traditional block Flock came to mind because it gives considerable design flexibility. I played with the color arrangement and put the blocks on point. The quilt *Misty Morn at Sunrise* was born.

Misty Morn at Sunrise, 26˝ × 26˝, designed by Joen Wolfrom, pieced and quilted by Mickie Swall.

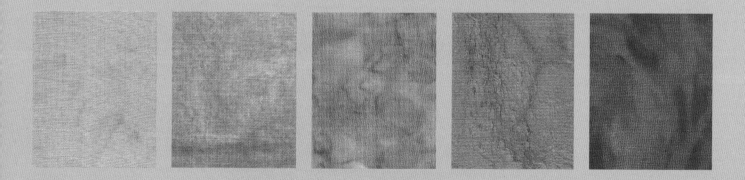

COLOR INSPIRATION: *The Last to Leave*

Sample 5: German Chocolate Cake

I was struck by the tenacity of these last leaves hanging on brilliantly as winter crept into the New Hampshire landscape one November morning. The soft golden leaves stood out strongly against the quiet backdrop of impending winter.

The contrast between the lonely leaves and the surrounding browns, rusts, and plums gave an unexpected beauty to explore. I chose a selection of fabrics from the colors in the photo, omitting the sky hues.

I sent the fabrics and photo to Patsy Preiss. Exploring numerous design possibilities, she opted to create a traditional charmer—a basket quilt. This wall quilt, *German Chocolate Cake*, is a wonderful reflection of the visual coloring from The Last to Leave photo.

German Chocolate Cake, 31″ × 31″, designed and pieced by Patsy Preiss, machine quilted by Kelly Edwards.

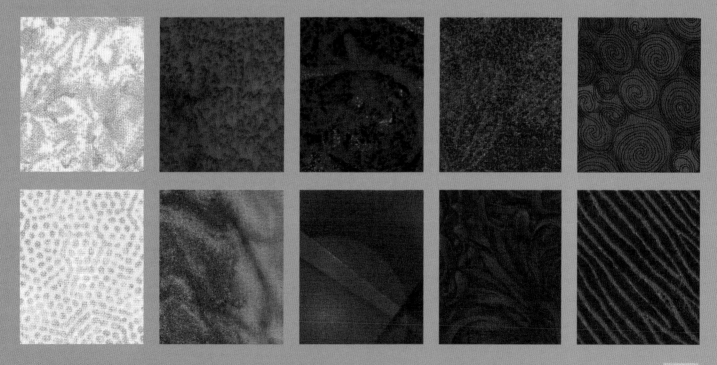

COLOR INSPIRATION: *Spring at Last*

Sample: 6: Irish Spring Garden

I love the unveiling of the hydrangea's petals when late spring arrives. The soft, delicate lavender seems to paint the edges of the petals, and the center is splashed with strongly colored yellow-greens. As summer appears, the green petals disappear, and the hydrangea is filled with beautiful red-violet blossoms that last the entire season. Through visual coloring, I chose fabrics for a new rendition of the traditional Double Irish Chain. Putting fabric to design, Mickie Swall created the quilt *Irish Spring Garden*.

Irish Spring Garden, 65″ × 81″, designed by Joen Wolfrom, pieced by Mickie Swall, machine quilted by Karen Dovala, bound by Joanne Williams.

Sample 7: Star Tiles

I rarely work in browns, so I found my interest in this photographic imagery perplexing. I finally concluded that I was intrigued by the strong value contrasts, the pronounced textures, and the extraordinarily subtle color changes of this bark photo.

Choosing fabrics from this image was amazing, because the hue range was quite diverse. I decided to focus on the soft, delicate hues of the image.

Star Tiles, is quite different in feel from Terri Palmer's quilt *Frenzied Arrangement* (page 57), which features the darker hues of the same image. It is hard to believe that these two quilts came from the same color-inspiration image.

COLOR INSPIRATION: *Tree Bark*

Star Tiles, 44″ × 44″, designed by Joen Wolfrom, pieced and quilted by Mickie Swall.

BEGINNING YOUR QUILT

When you begin thinking about your next quilting project, look at the color images you have collected in your files. Select the one that you respond to most powerfully. Put the remaining color images back in your files for another time. Then study your selected image, noticing the different hues and subtle color nuances in the picture. Enlarge the image if necessary.

Go to your fabric stash with your color-inspiration image and begin choosing fabrics in the same colors. You may want to choose fabrics with the most obvious colors first and then go back to choose fabrics from the less noticeable colorings; or just choose all your colors as you go.

If your stash is lacking in one or more areas, visit your local fabric store with your image in hand. You can see immediately which fabrics match the image and which don't. After gathering all of your fabrics, place them on your worktable and observe them from a distance (eight or ten feet). Take out any fabrics that are bothersome or don't seem to work well with the rest.

Once you have determined your quilt design, separate the fabrics into piles, indicating their placement in the design. Determine which fabrics and colors will be given a major role in the design, which ones will be secondary, which will be used as accents, and which ones will be used in the background. Once these steps have been completed, you are ready to begin constructing your quilt.

AN ENDING THOUGHT

As you can see, visual coloring allows you the freedom to work with colors you love. It helps you see clearly the color combinations you love to work in, and it gives you practical guidelines with which to work. The added benefit is that visual coloring is easy to use in making color and fabric choices.

All of the colors and fabrics used in the quilts included in this book were selected by visual coloring. The color-inspiration image is noted for each quilt. I hope you enjoy studying the fantastic display of quilts presented in *Visual Coloring*.

DO YOU WANT TO KNOW MORE ABOUT COLOR?

If you want to learn more about color, read my book *Color Play* and look at my *3-in-1 Color Tool*. In these sources, you will find basic information on color families, color scales, tints, shades, tones, values, color plans, and color illustrations.

ACTIVITIES AND EXERCISES

1. If you haven't already done so, take the time to begin building files of color images that you love. Keep the files close at hand so you can add to them and refer to them often.

2. Select one of the photos from this section to use for your own visual coloring exercise. Study its colors. Then take the photo to your fabric stash. Choose as many fabrics as you can from your collection. Place them on your worktable and stand back to assess the results. Discard any fabrics that seem out of place or distracting. Select another photo and repeat the exercise.

3. Many photographic images are shown throughout this book. Select the ones that you like most. One at a time, study the colors in each photo. Then take the book to your fabric stash and begin choosing fabrics from the colors you see. Repeat the process for each image.

4. Taking the fabrics you seem most drawn to from one of the above exercises, select a design and make a quilt using these fabrics.

5. If you love fall colors, choose fabrics from each of the photos on the facing page. You will find that the subtle differences between the colors in the photos will make a significant difference in the fabrics selected. Therefore, quilts made from each of these photos will be quite different even though they are all fall quilts.

This autumnal imagery feels happy and light with its yellows, golds, and soft ranges. The rich coppery hues and deep browns blend beautifully with the lighter colors.

The soft greens and yellow-green hues create a palette quite different from the others on this page. The light values and soft greens blend beautifully with the browns, rusts, and tans. A quilt made from this palette would be soft, warm, and quietly uplifting.

This impressionistic fall scene is more somber than the other images. The touch of olive could be used as an accent or completely eliminated. Deep rust, grayed beiges, and tan create a strong, rich mood. This coloring feels very masculine.

Irises Dressed in Blue, Judy Simmons,
Fletcher, North Carolina; 30″ × 28″,
machine appliquéd and quilted.

Judy loves nature and the beautiful colors
shown in the hydrangea photo. Her design
inspirations were from her garden and the
gardens in her neighborhood. Limiting her
color selection, Judy gave blue-violet the
lead in this design. She hand dyed and
painted her fabric, using MX fiber reactive
dyes. The background was quilted using
decorative threads.

Birds in the Hydrangea,
Kay L. Bachkai, Barto,
Pennsylvania; 46″ × 46″,
machine pieced, hand quilted.

Kay combined the hydrangea colors
beautifully with the traditional block
Birds in the Air to create a striking
contemporary design. Kay's interesting
layout, combined with her excellent use
of color and value, creates a wonderful
dimensional design. Her placement of dark
and light hues elicits the illusion of
highlights and shadows.

Endless Mountains, Sandra Lee Schuler,
Telford, Pennsylvania; 38″ × 38″,
machine pieced and quilted.

Using the traditional pattern Thousand
Pyramids, Sandy created this beautiful quilt
by lightening up the colors from the photo;
she expanded the value range to create
this wonderfully delicate design. The mountains seemingly disappear into the distance
because of the color, value, and tonal
placement of the fabrics.

Ebb and Flow,
Adrienne Lindsay Cannon,
Louisville, Colorado; 52″ × 35″,
machine pieced and appliquéd,
machine quilted.

Adrienne's exquisite design
explodes with beautiful color
blends and value changes. To
create the subtle nuances of
color and value, Adrienne dyed
her own fabrics. The idea for her
quilt came quickly, but the challenge of her project was finding
the colors in the photograph and
then finding them in light,
medium, and dark fabrics. Getting
just the right fabrics involved
trips to all the quilt shops in her
area and hand dying fabrics.

A winter sunrise is a wonderful color inspiration. Here, the subtle hues move from soft, warm pinks to strong blues with blue-violet as the most featured color. The blue hues of the peninsula are the strongest of all.

Winter Morning Sunrise,
Janice Richards Smith,
Vaughn, Washington; 45″ × 53″,
machine pieced and quilted.

Through the window, you can see the water, the hills beyond, and the lofty Mt. Rainier in soft hues, as well as the beginnings of a winter sunrise. The photo's colors not only reiterate many of the winter sunrise colors but also incorporate many of Janice's favorite colors. She used strong variations of nature's colors in this scene with the many pinks in the morning before the sun rises. The sky colors reflect in the dark waters below.

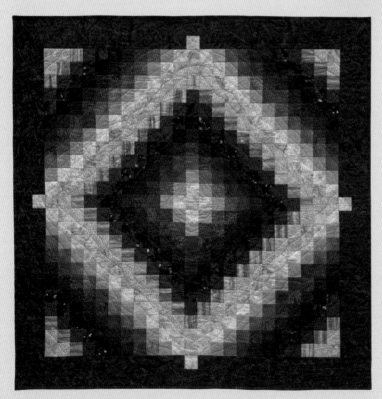

A Peaceful Trip Around the World,
Pat Raffee, Post Falls, Idaho;
55″ × 55″, machine pieced,
appliquéd, and quilted.

Pat interpreted the soothing quality of the winter sunrise photograph wonderfully in her beautiful Trip Around the World quilt. Pat chose to omit the warmest hues, using the coolest colors for her quilt.

COLOR INSPIRATION: *Hanging On*

I was intrigued by the wonderful richness the raindrops gave to the last few leaves hanging on an aspen tree in fall. I loved the coppery hues as they combined with the soft blue background with a hint of plum and soft green. Notice that the soft greens were not included in the quilt.

Pandora's Box, Joen Wolfrom, Fox Island, Washington; 32″ × 32″, machine pieced, machine quilted by Pat Harrison.

I loved working with this unusual coloring. The blending of the design and the fabrics reminded me of an intricately carved inlaid box.

Details of *My Field House Iris Garden*

Iris lovers can be found all over the world, rejoicing in the beauty of these flowers. Quilters who are also gardeners love to use irises for both color and design inspiration. Christine Porter created an exquisite iris quilt to excite our senses.

These exquisite irises are breathtaking. Chris used a myriad of gorgeously colored fabrics to create the iris petals. Each iris has its own rendition of color. This superb quilt reflects the beauty of its inspiration. Chris looked closely at the different shapes of the iris petals. She took the colors from the photos and used the background of greens and yellows for the background of the squares. Then she created irises in the same color theme as the petals in the photos.

In this quilt Christine wanted to capture the beauty and voluptuousness of irises. She chose fabric to match as closely as possible the original colors of the petals and leaves, and she fused the pieces straight onto the pieced background. The quilting thread closely matches the colors of the irises.

My Field House Iris Garden, Christine Porter, Bristol, England; 47″ × 59″, machine pieced and appliquéd, machine quilted. Photo by Neil Porter.

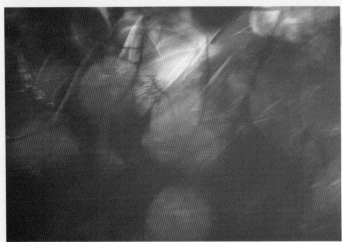

The brilliant dogwood berries dancing gloriously in the wind, are shown here with the blurred colorations of tree trunk, branches, leaves, and fruit, as well as bits of sky.

Fire Bowls, Patrice Creswell, Austin, Texas; 52˝ × 43˝, hand and machine pieced, appliquéd, and quilted.

Patrice created a textured richness in *Fire Bowls*, with its multiple techniques and wonderful color use. She not only expanded the range of color values, but she also created luster by subtly moving values from very light to dark-medium on the left side. Also, the play of dark, medium, and light values within the block shapes creates the illusion of shadows and highlights, as well as movement. Patrice's original design is wonderfully creative, combining Asian visuals with an asymmetrical border of the traditional pattern Winding Ways. When Patrice first looked at the photo, she saw only a few major colors. The more she examined the photo, the more colors jumped out at her.

Made in the Shade, Patrice Creswell, Austin, Texas; 82″ × 75″, hand and machine appliquéd, pieced, and quilted.

Using all the colors present in the dogwood berries photo, Patrice was able to present many visual vignettes. *Made in the Shade* should tickle your fancy with its many surprising details just awaiting discovery. Patrice broadened the value range of many of her colors, giving her more options. She created the illusion of depth beautifully by making certain that the foreground objects were strongly colored and that the objects in the background faded into lighter and grayer colorings.

COLOR INSPIRATION: *Forest Edge at Dusk*

The colors seem magical here as the sun shines at the forest edge on a Canadian spring evening. The brown tones seem almost unreal. The silver shimmers. The greens range from mossy to deep, dark bluish hues.

Nine-Patch Upgrade, Billie Mahorney, Lake Oswego, Oregon; 44″ × 44″, machine pieced and quilted.

Creating her own design using the photo colors as a guide, Billie increased the proportion of light values in her quilt. Also, she substituted strong rusts and dark oranges for the soft, grayed rusty hues in the photo.

Lilies in My Fish Pond, Bette Moyer, Pottstown, Pennsylvania; 52″ × 71″, pieced and appliquéd with raw-edge appliqué, machine quilted by Barbara Persing.

Lilies in My Fish Pond is a stunning explosion of color displayed in the popular tropical flower colors of the bird-of-paradise. The fish fabric in this quilt had been in Bette's stash for quite some time. She found that the bird-of-paradise photo worked perfectly with this fabric. She began pulling fabrics that worked with both the photo and the fish fabric. She used several purple fabrics for the background and many different greens for the leaves. Bette's design inspiration came from a block in Doreen Speckmann's book *Pattern Play*.

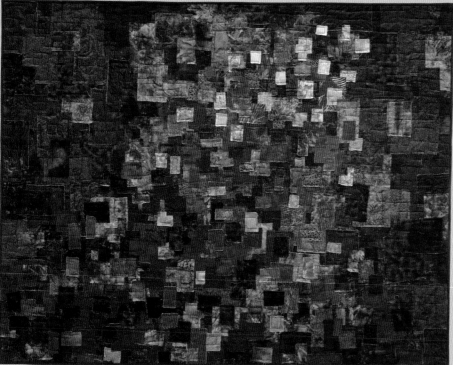

Avila Memories 1989, Nancy R. Board, Amherst, Massachusetts; 53″ × 41″, pieced and raw-edge machine appliquéd.

Using the brilliant coloring of the bird-of-paradise, Nancy created a fun, free-spirited contemporary design for her project. The foreground uses the strong flower colors, and the background quietly reflects the greenery.

COLOR INSPIRATION: *New Zealand Sunrise*

Sunrise is a beautiful time of day, as is exhibited in this image of the sunlight just beginning to break through the darkness.

COLOR INSPIRATION: *Bird-of-Paradise in the Garden*

The bird-of-paradise is such a glorious sight to those who love strong coloring. This flower presents quite a beautiful inspiration for visual coloring with its brilliant yellows, oranges, blue-violets, and hints of other colors.

Detail of *Life Circles*

Life Circles, Maria Lage, Cumberland, Rhode Island; 31″ × 34″, machine pieced, hand appliquéd, hand quilted.

Maria's breathtakingly beautiful quilt combines the colors of two photos. Her fabric selection is absolutely stunning with all the subtle color nuances. The quilt's background represents a beautiful tile wall, which, according to Maria, is an important feature in traditional Portuguese family homes. This tile wall is exquisitely hand appliquéd in the finest workmanship. The poppies, bread, and grapes depicted in this still life are symbolic of Maria's family.

This beautifully subtle rose elicits an analogous array of colors that blend so beautifully together. You can see the soft creams, yellows, apricots, peaches, corals, and rusty oranges in the rose.

First Light, Sally Collins, Walnut Creek, California; 15˝ × 15˝, machine pieced, hand and machine quilted.

Sally loved the colors in the rose picture, so she pulled fabrics from the photo to begin a basic palette. The design was still a mystery as she started this process. In the end, she selected the traditional LeMoyne Star and Festival blocks. Sally identified the colors in the inspiration piece (red-orange, yellow, green) and then expanded each color to include a range of values, visual textures, and intensities.

Ancient Symbols, Donna Shannon, Whitehall, Pennsylvania; 32″ × 32″, machine pieced, yarn crunching, machine quilted.

Donna's intriguing quilt was based on the pattern *Garden Maze* by Janet Pittman (*Love of Quilting* magazine, May–June 2003). Using many different greens and making this a paper-piecing project allowed Donna to create a unique variation on this design. She was drawn to the rose photo because it contained colors she had been collecting.

The Sky's the Limit, Lynn Lentz, Coopersburg, Pennsylvania; 32″ × 32″, machine pieced and quilted.

Lynn's lovely quilt was inspired by Annette Ornelas's Mexican Star pattern (published by Southwind Designs). The quilt's curved lines were created by turning back the folded triangle inserts and then topstitching. Lynn interpreted the rose in restful colors.

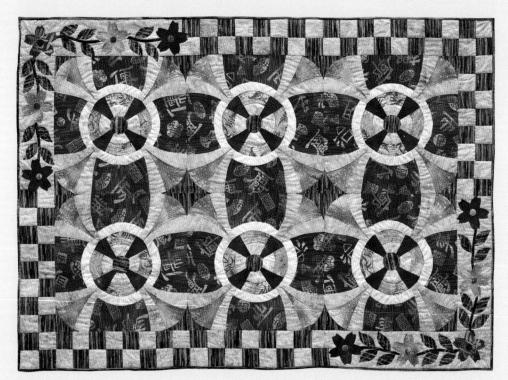

Cleopatra's Carpet, Sylvia Kundrats, Quakertown, Pennsylvania; 53 1/2″ × 38″, machine pieced, hand appliquéd, machine quilted by Barbara Persing.

The patterns for this quilt's flowers, checkerboard, and block (Cleopatra) came from the book *East Quilts West* by Kumiko Sudo. Sylvia's design reminds her of a carpet; hence the name *Cleopatra's Carpet*. Using nature as a guide, Sylvia created strong circular elements with the lightest lights against the darkest darks—each one being a focal point. The border flowers add a special touch to the design.

It is not necessary to have a clear, precise image for visual coloring. In fact, a blurred image forces you to concentrate on the colors rather than on the realism of the image, as you see in this wind-blown maple tree image.

An Autumn Adventure, Lois E. Dunten, La Grange, Indiana; 75″ × 93″, machine pieced, machine quilted by Colleen Gall.

Even though this autumnal photo was blurred, the vibrant colors were easily discernable for visual coloring. Lois created this stunning Trip Around the World quilt with 26 fabrics that she found in her own fabric collection—as well as several of her favorite quilt shops.

Pieceful Garden, Mary Sorensen, Longwood, Florida, and Jan Wildman, Orlando, Florida; 56″ × 56″, hand appliquéd, machine pieced, machine quilted.

This beautiful quilt was a collaborative design: Mary designed all of the appliqué elements, and Jan designed the pieced blocks. They collaborated on the borders and set. Jan quilted the design. The colors in this photo are the colors with which Mary is most comfortable. Because Jan was piecing leaves, she was committed to greens. Although most of Jan's greens were fairly strong, they were in a narrow value range. The narrow range made it easy for Mary to introduce more value contrast into the flower fabrics. Mary and Jan purposely chose toned versions of gold and green for the outer border of the quilt in a very narrow value range, so the border would act as an ending rather than as a frame.

Because the colors in this quiet fall image are very closely related, value becomes an important factor.

Autumn Breeze, Barbara Persing, Frederick, Pennsylvania; 72″ × 85″, machine pieced and appliquéd, machine quilted.

Barbara's *Autumn Breeze* is filled with wonderful subtle surprises, as falling leaves seem to float throughout the quilt onto the forest floor. Her design is accentuated by closely related values and hues. The leaves look like beautiful gems on the fading fall colors.

This lovely scene is filled with wonderful fall colors, providing the potential for a stunning quilt using visual coloring to pull colors and fabrics.

Autumn Star, Patsy Preiss, Rockton, Illinois; 71˝ × 71˝; machine pieced, machine quilted by Kelly Edwards.

With a selection of fabrics in colors pulled from this fall image, Patsy created a beautiful Lone Star quilt. The star is wonderfully accentuated by the pieced border in matching fabrics. Kelly Edwards enhanced the star with her exquisite quilting.

Mossy Tree Limb in Snow

Tree Bark

Winter Trees

Star Magnolia Bud in Snow

The color inspiration for Cassandra Williams's magnificent quilt *Bullseye!* comes from the five photos shown here.

Red Branches in Snow

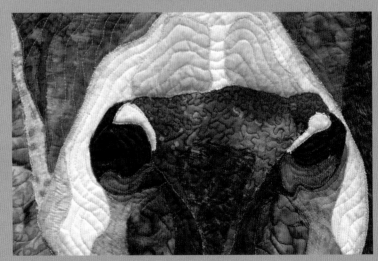

Details of *Bullseye!*

Bullseye! Cassandra Williams, Grants Pass, Oregon; 62″ × 72″, designed, created, and quilted by Cassandra Williams.

This magnificent quilt depicting Frankie the bull uses colors from five winter-hued photos. From the photos selected, Cassandra began by pulling cream, chocolate, charcoal, and a little soft salmon. She added the soft winter greens, as well as many other hues to give the needed subtle contrasts. In addition, her exquisite color use provides depth and evokes sensitivity and emotion. Also, you can see the majestic strength and personality of Frankie the bull. Cassandra was able to convey many different colors in the bull's coat by using raw-edge appliqué with free-motion quilting.

Our much-loved star magnolia bush anticipates spring in the deep of winter. Its fuzzy, swollen buds reiterate the quietness of the season, as it awaits its massive presentation of white blossoms. Pulling colors from this photo gives a palette of quiet earthiness.

Low Tide, an extraordinary quilt, is a fascinating study in value. The design was created from Helene's memories of tidal marshes on foggy mornings from her childhood days along the central California coast.

Helene used a wide value range to give contrast within the design. Also, she shifted the photo's value ratio to use more of the light frosty colors and less of the dark background tones. The ratio is reversed by almost fifty percent. The details created by the multitude of textured fabrics, as well as the variation of quilting stitches throughout the surface design, make this a breathtaking quilt with exquisite subtleties.

Low Tide, Helene Knott, Oregon City, Oregon; 64˝ × 90˝, machine pieced, appliquéd, and quilted.

At first only the dark brown, charcoal, and beige are noticeable. However, as your eyes acclimate, other hues are found.

Kenya Cottonstainers, Karla Harris, Hope, Idaho; 31″ × 60¹/₂″, hand and machine pieced and appliquéd with beading, couching, and embroidery, machine quilted by Nona Harris King.

The quiet colors in the photo used for visual coloring appear to be an unlikely inspiration for this very clever quilt featuring happy insects with endearing personalities. This quilt was a personal challenge for Karla because she used techniques and accessories she had never used before—netting, tulle, yarns and threads, modified trapunto, and couching.

This tree bark gives subtle color blends, wide value ranges, and superb textures.

Frenzied Arrangement, Terri Palmer, Sand Point, Idaho; 23″ × 38″, hand and machine pieced, hand quilted.

This whimsical flower arrangement is beautifully created with the subtle hues from tree bark. The quilt's value key is much darker than the photo image's light key. Terri's quilting includes sewn seed beads. The values and hues are very subtle. This quilt is filled with many interesting and creative details.

The breath of winter brings a mantle of soft toned colors, which give quilters the opportunity to work with quiet hues. This photo offers many surprising hues—soft mossy green, pale blue, browns, warm taupe, and hints of lavender all present themselves.

Viva, Violas, Judy Simmons, Fletcher, North Carolina; 22″ × 28″, machine appliquéd and quilted.

Judy loves to use nature as a theme in her artworks. She is fascinated by nature's colors and textures. Using visual coloring, Judy pulled the subtle hues from this quiet winter scene to create a lovely, understated magical viola garden.

Global Warning, Terri Palmer, Sand Point, Idaho; 26″ × 32″, hand and machine appliquéd, machine quilted by Nona Harris King.

The very subtle colors, derived from the hues of this winter tree limb, create this parched-earth art piece of dry creek bed, hills, and sky. The majority of fabric in *Global Warning* is raw silk that was hand dyed by Terri.

As winter arrives, hydrangeas fade into beautiful toned hues with each hydranga having its own subtle changes. This hydrangea was the color inspiration for these two very different quilts.

Graciella, Nancy J. Deputy, Quakertown, Pennsylvania; 36″ × 36″, machine and hand pieced, hand quilted.

Nancy celebrates the colors of this hydrangea in her striking traditional quilt *Graciella*. The hydrangea photo contained unexpected hues. Visual coloring helped Nancy see colors that she had not noticed at first glance. Her use of the dark green in the shadows, in contrast with the beautiful warm rose, gives her design a very strong, rich effect. Nancy's design was an adaptation of a pattern in Carol Doak's book *Easy Machine Paper Piecing*.

Last One, Nona Harris King, Greenacres, Washington; 62″ × 75″, machine pieced and quilted.

Nona selected quiet hues from her selected photo, keeping the values close in contrast. The shapes in this design work beautifully in this quilt because they reiterate the shapes of the hydrangea blossoms. She used the pattern Spring Fever from the book *Certifiably Crazy* by Buggy Barn. Nona loved the ease of pulling fabrics by matching the colors in the photo. She didn't even check whether the fabrics matched each other. If they matched the photo, they were in.

Star Flower Medallion,
Mickie Swall, Cranberry Township,
Pennsylvania; 28″ × 28″, machine
appliquéd, machine quilted.

Mickie chose to use
strong pinks and greens to
play the lead role in this
happy appliqué quilt. The
more subtle hues pulled
from the photo are cleverly
arranged in narrow pieces
around the center medallion.

This wild foxglove photo is
filled with soft, gentle greens, pinks,
and lavenders. Impressionistic
images work well with visual
coloring because they allow for
subtle color nuances.

At first glance, you may be taken with the
strong cerise petals in a sea of green leaves.
However, as your eyes begin to explore further,
you will see the delicate coloring of the
blossom bottoms and the strong colors at the
tips of the bleeding heart blossoms.

Hybrid Lily, Betty Kegerreis-Fulmer, Quakertown, Pennsylvania; 42″ × 33″, machine pieced and appliquéd.

Betty's *Hybrid Lily* takes advantage of all the different colorings from the bleeding
heart photo. The daylily bloom uses the strongest colors in the bleeding heart blossoms.
Betty used a beautiful arrangement of greens. She cleverly took the soft palette of the
blossoms for her background. To quiet the effect, Betty used fabrics in slightly grayed
colors (tones). The strong hues of the flower and the leaves set against soft, grayed
background hues creates wonderful dimension (depth) in this quilt.

COLOR INSPIRATION: *Heliconia Dressed in Red*

The beautiful hues of this heliconia
create wonderful color options. The blurred
background offers a hint of blue, which
can be used or ignored.

Working by hand from drafting to quilting, Stacie made this lovely traditional Double
Wedding Ring quilt with more than a hundred fabrics. The hues and the value changes in
the heliconia photo gave Stacie great opportunity to work with value, contrast, and color.
The fresh colors of spring yellow-greens, cool reds, and warm blues from the photo were the
color inspiration for this quilt.

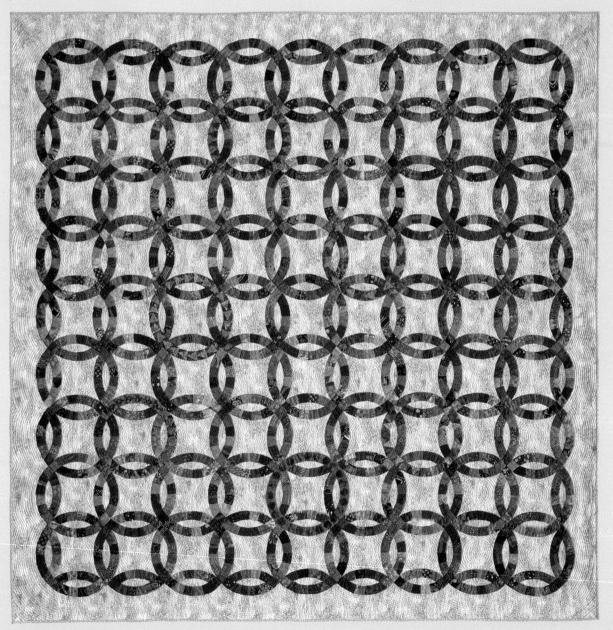

An Old-Fashioned Spring Wedding, Stacie Littlejohn, Wallacetown, Ontario, Canada; 70˝ × 70˝, hand pieced and appliquéd, hand quilted.

This heliconia in its sunny background gives a quilter the option to create a design with strong value contrast between foreground and background.

Shadows of the Heliconia, Judith B. Rumpf, Quakertown, Pennsylvania; 51″ × 51″, machine pieced, quilted by Barbara Persing.

Using the tropical colors inspired by the heliconia, Judy created this very spirited traditional-style quilt. The variation of greens, reddish-pinks, and corals is ever so subtle. The book *Shadow Quilts* by Donna Slusser and Patricia Magaret was the design source and inspiration for Judy's quilt.

Invasion of the Osmundas Regalis, Stacie Littlejohn, Wallacetown, Ontario, Canada; 56″ × 38″, machine appliquéd and quilted.

Being a gardener and loving nature's subtleties, Stacie chose this tropical flower photo as her color inspiration for her featured plant, the fern. She then abstracted, simplified, and enlarged a less noticeable part of the fern. The seed for this quilt was sown in Jane Sassaman's workshop Abstracting from Nature. The fresh yellow-greens, cool reds, and warm blues from the photo were the color inspiration for this quilt.

COLOR INSPIRATION: *Rejoicing Gerberas*

The subtle hues of this gerbera, as well as the bright background greens, are perfect for creating bright, happy quilts.

Pennsylvania German Fraktur,
Kathleen A. Wydrzynski,
Boyertown, Pennsylvania; 24″ × 38″,
machine pieced and hand appliquéd,
hand quilted.

Kathleen loves red, so she chose the colors from the gerbera picture for her quilt. Living in an area that is richly steeped in German heritage, Kathleen chose a design that reflected this culture. Kathleen used a pattern designed by Lydia Quigley (The Rabbit Factory).

COLOR INSPIRATION: *Woodland Floor*

The woodland floor is filled with earthy rich colors from which to select a great number of colors.

Trip to California, Ellen Inghrim,
Hellertown, Pennsylvania; 37″ × 47″,
machine pieced, hand appliquéd, hand
quilted, hand embroidered.

Ellen designed a quilt that used a variation of the traditional block Road to California. Visual coloring allowed her to use a large selection of colors to make this happy quilt.

This stormy evening provides great color inspiration with its analogous colors that move from very dark brownish-plum to orange to golden yellow. The possibilities for striking designs are unlimited.

Sunrise, Sunset, Karla Harris, Hope, Idaho; 100˝ × 100˝, machine pieced, machine quilted by Nona Harris King.

This unique Log Cabin design makes a beautiful arrangement for the color play in this quilt. Karla ever so subtly combined all of the colors from this evocative sunset for her quilt's design. This quilt was inspired by a quilt in the book *Log Cabin in the Round Designs* by Barbara Schaffeld and Bev Vickery.

COLOR INSPIRATION: *Night Glow*

You don't have to limit yourself to nature scenes when searching for color inspiration. Here, the dramatic glowing yellows of the tiki torch blend into the reddish-oranges, which in turn move into deep plums and blackened red-violets.

Ar Thine, Mary Hoover, Ballston Lake, New York; 60″ × 86″, machine pieced, hand quilted.

Using the brilliant night glow of the tiki torch for her color inspiration, Mary chose to put a modern twist on the traditional Trip Around the World design. *Ar Thine* absolutely vibrates with dynamic color as it moves from the brightest yellow to the deepest plums and dark browns.

COLOR INSPIRATION: *Tree Peony in Bloom*

The beautiful array of hues exhibited in this magnificent tree peony blossom offers a wonderful color palette.

A Blossom for Beth, Kandice J. Carnahan, Gig Harbor, Washington; 50″ × 42″, machine pieced, machine quilted by Jacque Noard.

Kandice interpreted the colors of the tree peony so that they move throughout her design as they do in the photo. She used a traditional-style design in a very contemporary mode.

PROJECT 1: Autumn Log Cabin

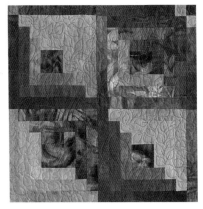

Autumn is a glorious time of year. A beautiful tree filled with riotous colors gives wonderful color inspiration for a quilt, even as the wind blows. Golden yellows, oranges, rusts, burnt oranges, burnt reds, maroons or plummy reds, chartreuses, warm browns, and a variety of greens all can be pulled from this one glorious fall image.

Uncharacteristically, I used only eighteen fabrics for this quilt. You can limit your fabric use or make a marvelous scrappy quilt by incorporating dozens of fabrics. The fabrics used in the project quilt *Autumn Log Cabin* are shown on page 70.

KING-SIZE BED QUILT

Skill Level: Confident beginner
Number of Blocks: 144
Finished Block Size: 8″

Autumn Log Cabin, 106 ¹/₂″ × 106 ¹/₂″, designed by Joen Wolfrom, pieced by Mickie Swall, machine quilted by Karen Dovala, bound by Joanne Williams.

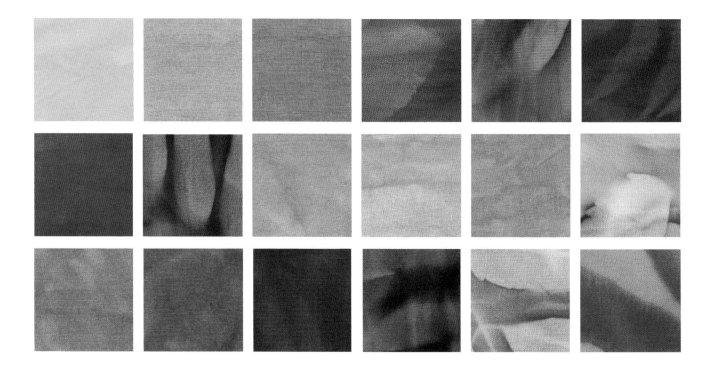

Thoughts About Fabric

Use fabrics that evoke the feelings of fall, from warm greens to chartreuses, golden yellows, coppers, oranges, and reds. Include rusts, warm browns, and plummy reds or maroons. Select a featured fabric that includes the widest possible range in your color selection. If possible, feature a leafy print. If you can't find such a print, use another motif that elicits a feeling of fall. This fabric will be repeated throughout the design and is featured in the quilt's center, so pick a fabric you really love. I chose a strong leafy fabric that moved through the entire range of my quilt's colors. The large color range provides a backdrop for many colors. I have included two swatches of this fabric, because the hues vary greatly from one area to another.

TIP

Here are a few simple guidelines for getting the look you want for your traditionally cut and pieced Log Cabin blocks:

- The color or value of the first 2 strips you add to the center square will finish on the outer edge of the block, but *not* at the outermost tip of the quilt.

- The color or value of the second 2 strips you add will finish on the outer edge of the block *and* be the color or value that finishes at the outermost tip. In a traditional setting, this side of the block will appear the most dominant.

- Be sure to sew an accurate and consistent $1/4''$ seam allowance. The Log Cabin block has multiple seams, and inconsistent stitching will quickly alter the block size.

- Carefully press each seam away from the block center as you go. Use a dry iron to keep your blocks from stretching.

- Chain piecing speeds the stitching process. I usually chain piece 4–8 blocks at a time.

FABRIC REQUIREMENTS

Yardages are based on 40˝-wide fabric (after washing).

Fabric A: 5¼ yards autumn-colored large-scale leaf print for blocks and outer border

Fabric B: 1⅝ yards (total) assorted light to medium yellow, gold, and yellow-orange hand-dyed fabrics or tone-on-tone prints for blocks

Fabric C: 1¾ yards (total) assorted medium to medium-dark copper, warm tan, and rust hand-dyed fabrics or tone-on-tone prints for blocks

Fabric D: 1⅜ yards (total) assorted medium to medium-dark green hand-dyed fabrics or tone-on-tone prints for blocks

Fabric E: 1⅞ yards (total) assorted light to light-medium yellow-green hand-dyed fabrics or tone-on-tone prints for blocks

Fabric F: 1½ yards (total) assorted medium-dark orange large-scale tone-on-tone leaf prints for blocks

Fabric G: ⅔ yard (total) assorted light-medium yellow-green large-scale tone-on-tone leaf prints for blocks

Inner Border: 2⅞ yards medium-dark green hand-dyed fabric or tone-on-tone print

Binding: 1⅛ yards

Backing: 9⅓ yards

Batting: 112˝ × 112˝ piece

CUTTING

Measurements include ¼˝ seam allowances. Cut strips on the crosswise grain of the fabric (selvage to selvage) unless instructed otherwise.

* From the *lengthwise grain* of Fabric A, cut:
- 2 strips, 4˝ × 99½˝
- 2 strips, 4˝ × 106½˝
- 4 strips, 2½˝ × 106½˝; crosscut into 144 squares, 2½˝ × 2½˝

* Divide this fabric crosswise into 2 pieces before you begin cutting: 1 piece 110˝ long and 1 piece 79˝ long.

From the remaining Fabric A, cut:
- 51 strips, 1½˝ × 40˝

From Fabric B, cut *a total of*:
- 36 strips, 1½˝ × 40˝

From Fabric C, cut *a total of*:
- 39 strips, 1½˝ × 40˝

From Fabric D, cut *a total of*:
- 29 strips, 1½˝ × 40˝

From Fabric E, cut *a total of*:
- 41 strips, 1½˝ × 40˝

From Fabric F, cut *a total of*:
- 33 strips, 1½˝ × 40˝

From Fabric G, cut *a total of*:
- 14 strips, 1½˝ × 40˝

From the *lengthwise grain* of the inner-border fabric, cut:
- 2 strips, 2˝ × 96½˝
- 2 strips, 2˝ × 99½˝

From the binding fabric, cut:
- 12 strips, 3¼˝ × 40˝ (double-fold binding sewn with ½˝ seam; finishes about ½˝ wide)

LOG CABIN BLOCK

Arrows indicate pressing direction.
You need 144 Log Cabin blocks. All blocks are constructed in the same way with the same fabric for the center square (Fabric A); only the coloration of the strips changes. You will need 4 Block 1 (B and A), 8 Block 2 (C and D), 20 Block 3 (E and A), 16 Block 4 (D and A), 20 Block 5 (C and B), 24 Block 6 (D, F, and G), 20 Block 7 (C and E), 16 Block 8 (B and A), 12 Block 9 (E and F), and 4 Block 10 (E, F, and G).

Block 1

1. Sew a 1½˝-wide Fabric B strip to the right edge of a 2½˝ Fabric A square. Press. Trim the strip even with the edge of the square. Make 4.

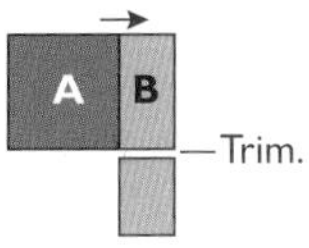

Make 4.

2. Sew a 1½˝-wide matching Fabric B strip to the bottom edge of each unit from Step 1. Press. Trim the strip even with the edge of the square.

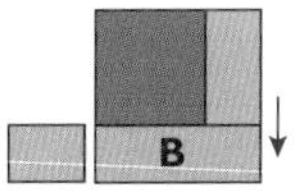

3. Sew a 1½˝-wide Fabric A strip to the left edge of each unit from Step 2. Press. Trim the strip even with the edge of the square.

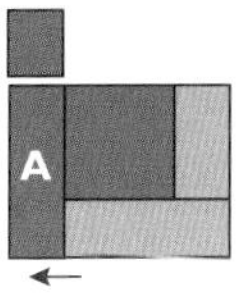

4. Sew a 1½˝-wide Fabric A strip to the top edge of each unit from Step 3. Press. Trim the strip even with the edge of the unit.

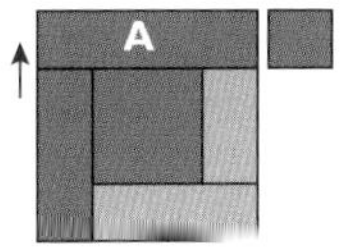

North Wind: Flora in the Furrows

COLOR INSPIRATION: *Hydrangea in Summer*

For those who love blue-violet (or periwinkle),
this hydrangea imagery is a dream come true.

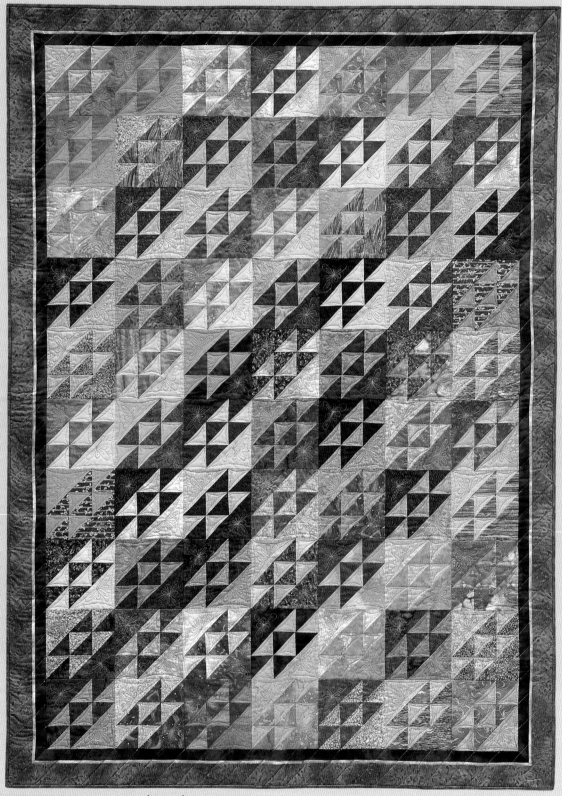

North Wind: Flora in the Furrows, 48$\frac{1}{2}$" × 66$\frac{1}{2}$", made by Lois E. Dunten. This lovely quilt was inspired by the "field and furrows" setting shown in Sharyn Squier Craig's book *Design Challenge: Northwind Quilts*.

LARGE WALL/LAP QUILT

Skill Level: Confident beginner

Number of Blocks: 70

Finished Block Size: 6"

PROJECT 3: Star Bright, Snow White

The sky is such an important part of the day because it sets the mood. Blue skies with wispy white clouds floating through the air are magical. This combination seems perfect for refreshingly cool star quilts.

If you really study white clouds, you will see that they are actually subtly colored. You may see some pink or lavender. I chose to ignore those hints of color. Instead I interpreted the sky and clouds literally and worked only with blue and white. All of the fabrics I used are shown in the swatches here.

The sky is such an important part of the day...

Star Bright, Snow White, 55½″ × 55½″, designed by Joen Wolfrom, pieced by Mickie Swall, machine quilted by Gayla Burger, bound by Joanne Williams.

LARGE WALL/LAP QUILT

Skill Level: Confident beginner

Number of Star Blocks: 13

Number of Snow Blocks: 12

Finished Block Size: 9″

Thoughts About Fabric

When I designed this quilt, I envisioned stars and snow. I searched for blue fabrics with snowflake motifs. Luckily, I found two to fit my theme. The other blue fabrics were mostly tone-on-tone or textured fabrics in medium to dark values. One was a muted, medium blue polka dot fabric. If you are unable to find blue snowflake fabrics or subtle polka dot fabric, opt for more blue tone-on-tone fabrics or something with a subtle geometric print. There should be subtle value changes in these fabrics. Six white textured fabrics—each a little different from the others—were used in the background. A white fabric with soft blue flowers was used in the middle border. This middle-border fabric could have been replaced by one of the white fabrics, which would look very nice in that position.

FABRIC REQUIREMENTS

Yardages are based on 40˝-wide fabric (after washing).

Fabric A: $1^3/4$ yards dark blue tone-on-tone print for Star blocks and outer border

Fabric B: $1^3/8$ yards (total) assorted white tone-on-tone prints for Star and Snow blocks*

Fabric C: $1^3/4$ yards medium blue snowflake print 1 for Star blocks and inner border

Fabric D: $1/3$ yard medium-dark blue tone-on-tone print for Snow blocks

Fabric E: $1/3$ yard light blue-on-white print for Snow blocks*

Fabric F: $1/3$ yard dark blue geometric print for Snow blocks

Fabric G: $1/4$ yard medium blue snowflake print 2 for Snow blocks

Fabric H: $1/3$ yard light-medium blue polka dot for Snow blocks

Fabric I: $1/4$ yard medium blue tone-on-tone print 1 for Snow blocks

Fabric J: $1/4$ yard medium blue tone-on-tone print 2 for Snow blocks

Middle Border: $1^3/4$ yards white tone-on-tone print

Binding: $2/3$ yard

Backing: $3^1/2$ yards

Batting: 61˝ × 61˝ piece

You may use 1 of these fabrics for the middle border.

CUTTING

Measurements include $1/4$˝ seam allowances. Cut strips on the crosswise grain of the fabric (selvage to selvage) unless instructed otherwise. Make templates for piece 1 and piece 2 using the patterns on page 83.

From the *lengthwise grain* of Fabric A, cut:
- 4 strips, $3^1/4$˝ × 60˝

From the remaining Fabric A, cut:
- 52 *each* piece 1 and piece 1 reverse using the template

From Fabric B, cut *a total of*:
- 13 piece 2 using the template*
- 52 squares, $3^1/2$˝ × $3^1/2$˝*
- 48 rectangles, 2˝ × $3^1/2$˝, in matching sets of 4**
- 48 squares, $2^3/8$˝ × $2^3/8$˝; cut once diagonally to make 2 half-square triangles (96 total)**

Cut these in matching sets of four $3^1/2$˝ squares and 4 piece 2 triangles.

**Cut these in matching sets of four 2˝ × $3^1/2$˝ rectangles and eight $2^3/8$˝ half-square triangles.*

From the *lengthwise grain* of Fabric C, cut:
- 4 strips, 2˝ × 60˝

From the remaining Fabric C, cut:
- 13 squares, $3^1/2$˝ × $3^1/2$˝

From Fabric D, cut:
- 2 strips, $3^1/2$˝ × 40˝; crosscut into 12 squares, $3^1/2$˝ × $3^1/2$˝

From Fabric E, cut:
- 5 strips, 2˝ × 40˝; crosscut into 48 rectangles, 2˝ × $3^1/2$˝

From Fabric F, cut:
- 5 strips, 2˝ × 40˝; crosscut into 96 squares, 2˝ × 2˝

From Fabric G, cut:
- 3 strips, 2˝ × 40˝; crosscut into 48 squares, 2˝ × 2˝

From Fabric H, cut:
- 3 strips, $2^3/8$˝ × 40˝; crosscut into 48 squares, $2^3/8$˝ × $2^3/8$˝; cut once diagonally to make 2 half-square triangles (96 total)

From Fabric I, cut:
- 2 strips, $2^3/8$˝ × 40˝; crosscut into 24 squares, $2^3/8$˝ × $2^3/8$˝; cut once diagonally to make 2 half-square triangles (48 total)

From Fabric J, cut:
- 2 strips, $2^3/8'' \times 40''$; crosscut into 24 squares, $2^3/8'' \times 2^3/8''$; cut once diagonally to make 2 half-square triangles (48 total)

From the *lengthwise grain* of the middle-border fabric, cut:
- 4 strips, $1^1/4'' \times 60''$

From the binding fabric, cut:
- 6 strips, $3^1/4'' \times 40''$ (double-fold binding sewn with $1/2''$ seam; finishes about $1/2''$ wide)

STAR BLOCK

You need 13 Star blocks for this quilt. Each block is made up of Fabric A, 1 Fabric B, and Fabric C. Instructions are for 1 block.

1. Sew Fabric A piece 1 and piece 1 reverse triangles to opposite sides of a Fabric B piece 2 triangle as shown. Press. Make 4 matching units.

Make 4.

2. Sew a unit from Step 1 between 2 matching $3^1/2''$ Fabric B squares as shown. Press. Make 2.

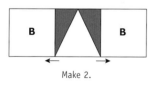

Make 2.

3. Sew a $3^1/2''$ Fabric C square between the 2 remaining units from Step 1 as shown. Press.

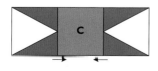

4. Sew the unit from Step 3 between the units from Step 2 as shown. Press.

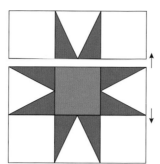

5. Repeat Steps 1–4 to make a total of 13 blocks.

SNOW BLOCK

You need 12 Snow blocks for this quilt. Each block is made up of 1 Fabric B and Fabrics D–J. Instructions are for 1 block.

1. Draw a diagonal line on the wrong side of two 2″ Fabric F squares.

2. Align a marked 2″ Fabric F square with the left edge of a $2'' \times 3^1/2''$ Fabric E rectangle, right sides together, as shown. Sew directly on the marked line and trim, leaving a $1/4''$ seam allowance. Press. Make 4.

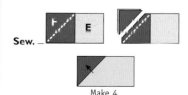

Sew.

Make 4.

3. Repeat Step 2 to sew a 2″ Fabric F square to the right edge of each unit. Trim and press. Make 4.

Make 4.

4. Sew a matching $2'' \times 3^1/2''$ Fabric B rectangle to each unit from Step 3. Press. Make 4.

Make 4.

5. Sew a $3^1/2''$ Fabric D square between 2 units from Step 4 as shown. Press.

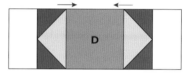

6. Sew $2^3/8''$ Fabric H and matching $2^3/8''$ Fabric B triangles together as shown. Press. Make 8.

Make 8.

7. Sew $2^3/8''$ Fabric I and Fabric J triangles together as shown. Press. Make 4.

Make 4.

8. Arrange 2 units from Step 6, a unit from Step 7, and a 2″ Fabric G square as shown. Sew the units and squares together into rows. Press. Sew the rows together. Press. Make 4.

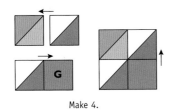

Make 4.

9. Sew 1 remaining unit from Step 4 between 2 units from Step 8 as shown. Press. Make 2.

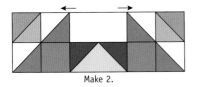

Make 2.

10. Sew the unit from Step 5 between the units from Step 9 as shown. Press.

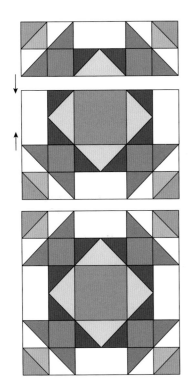

11. Repeat Steps 1–10 to make a total of 12 blocks.

QUILT ASSEMBLY

Arrows indicate pressing direction.

1. Refer to the assembly diagram and arrange the blocks in 5 horizontal rows of 5 blocks each, alternating the blocks as shown.

2. Sew the blocks into rows. Press the seams in opposite directions from row to row.

3. Sew the rows together.

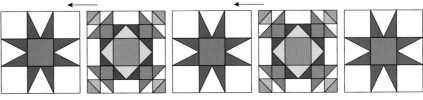

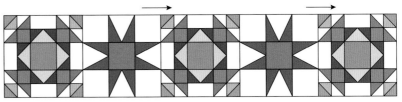

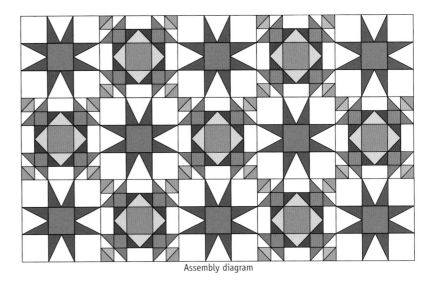

Assembly diagram

4. Sew a 2″ × 60″ Fabric C inner-border strip, a 1¼″ × 60″ middle-border strip, and a 3¼″ × 60″ Fabric A outer-border strip together to make a border unit as shown. Press. Make 4 and sew 2 of them to opposite sides of the quilt center. Sew the remaining 2 border units to the top and bottom. Miter the corners and press the seams away from the quilt center.

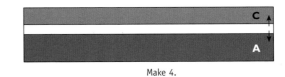

Make 4.

Finishing Steps

If you need help with the finishing process of layering, basting, marking your quilting design, quilting, and binding, refer to your favorite how to book or to the technical books I have recommended in References (page 94). Otherwise, layer, baste, mark, quilt, and bind in your preferred manner.

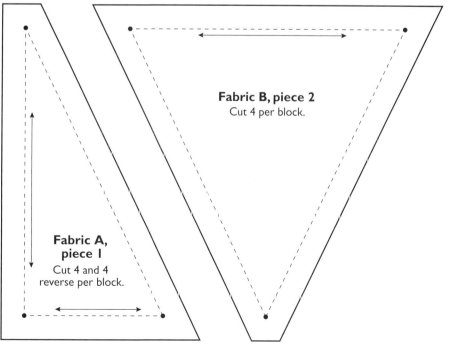

Fabric A, piece 1
Cut 4 and 4 reverse per block.

Fabric B, piece 2
Cut 4 per block.

PROJECT 4: Sunrise Lattice Stars

A sunrise welcomes us to the day, oftentimes exhibiting serene beauty. Every day brings a different color show. Being near a body of water at this time of day is an added bonus because the colors play wonderfully in the water too. This sunrise in the Rockies gives a lovely color combination of soft blues and coppery tans, warm browns, and golden apricots. As your eyes adjust to the image, even hints of lavender appear. If the darkest hues in this image seem to distract, do not use them. However, if you would like a design with highly contrasting values, include these dark hues.

The fabrics I pulled from this image are shown on page 86. I used only a few fabrics, but it would have been easy to include many more, thereby making this a scrappy quilt. I eliminated the strong dark foreground colors from the sunrise image.

Sunrise Lattice Stars, 42^1/$_2$″ × 42^1/$_2$″, designed by Joen Wolfrom, pieced and machine quilted by Mickie Swall.

WALL QUILT

Skill Level: Confident beginner

Number of Blocks: 9

Finished Block Size: 12″

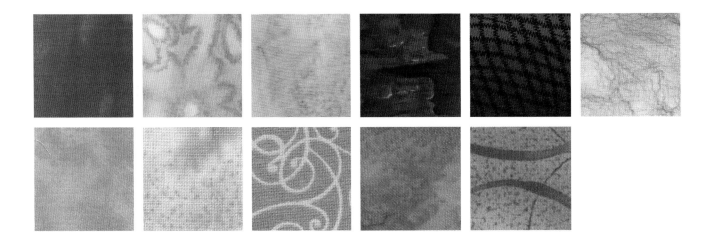

Thoughts About Fabric

This lattice design has a hidden star in its makeup. This star-point lattice is made from one dark rusty-brown textured fabric. The center of the lattice star is a warm coppery-tan fabric. Alternating with the star are large squares, which are made from a striped fabric. The stripe was oriented in the same direction from square to square. If you use a stripe, you can do the same, or you can alternate the stripes—whichever suits your fancy. I used two apricot tone-on-tone fabrics for the small light squares. The background was made from a selection of several blue fabrics. One had a hint of soft lavender in it, as the photo does. You can use fabrics similar to those I have chosen or make completely different choices. If you can't find a subtle striped fabric that you like, choose another fabric with wonderful texture or pattern interest.

FABRIC REQUIREMENTS

Yardages are based on 40˝-wide fabric (after washing).

Fabric A: ³/₄ yard dark rusty-brown subtle or tone-on-tone print for blocks

Fabric B: 1 yard (total) assorted light-medium to medium blue subtle or tone-on-tone prints for blocks

Fabric C: 1⁵/₈ yards warm tan subtle or tone-on-tone print for blocks and border

Fabric D: ¹/₄ yard *each* of 2 different apricot subtle or tone-on-tone prints for blocks

Fabric E: ¹/₃ yard light brown to dark brown variegated wavy stripe for blocks

Fabric F: ¹/₄ yard medium blue subtle or tone-on-tone print for flat mock piping *

Binding: ⁵/₈ yard

Backing: 2²/₃ yards

Batting: 48˝ × 48˝ piece

* *This may be 1 of the Fabric B prints.*

The sunrise in the Rockies gives a lovely color combination of soft blues and coppery tans, warm browns, and golden apricots.

CUTTING

Measurements include ¼″ seam allowances. Cut strips on the crosswise grain of the fabric (selvage to selvage) unless instructed otherwise.

From Fabric A, cut:
- 5 strips, $2\frac{1}{2}″ \times 40″$; crosscut into 72 squares, $2\frac{1}{2}″ \times 2\frac{1}{2}″$
- 3 strips, $2\frac{7}{8}″ \times 40″$; crosscut into 36 squares, $2\frac{7}{8}″ \times 2\frac{7}{8}″$; cut once diagonally to make 2 half-square triangles (72 total)

From Fabric B, cut *a total of*:
- 36 rectangles, $2\frac{1}{2}″ \times 4\frac{1}{2}″$
- 36 squares, $2\frac{7}{8}″ \times 2\frac{7}{8}″$; cut once diagonally to make 2 half-square triangles (72 total)
- 36 squares, $2\frac{1}{2}″ \times 2\frac{1}{2}″$

From the *lengthwise grain* of Fabric C, cut:
- 4 strips, $3\frac{1}{2}″ \times 48″$

From the remaining Fabric C, cut:
- 36 rectangles, $2\frac{1}{2}″ \times 4\frac{1}{2}″$
- 18 squares, $2\frac{7}{8}″ \times 2\frac{7}{8}″$; cut once diagonally to make 2 half-square triangles (36 total)

From *each* Fabric D, cut:
- 1 strip, $2\frac{7}{8}″ \times 40″$; crosscut into 9 squares, $2\frac{7}{8}″ \times 2\frac{7}{8}″$; cut once diagonally to make 2 half-square triangles (18 total from each fabric)

From Fabric E, cut:
- 2 strips, $4\frac{1}{2}″ \times 40″$; crosscut into 9 squares, $4\frac{1}{2}″ \times 4\frac{1}{2}″$*

* Cut these squares so that the value change appears in the same position in each square.

From Fabric F, cut:
- 5 strips, $\frac{3}{4}″ \times 40″$

From the binding fabric, cut:
- 5 strips, $3\frac{1}{4}″ \times 40″$ (double-fold binding sewn with $\frac{1}{2}″$ seam; finishes about $\frac{1}{2}″$ wide)

STAR LATTICE BLOCK

You need 9 blocks for this quilt. Fabrics A, C, and E and the 2 D Fabrics remain the same in each block. Each block also includes a scrappy mix of Fabric B prints. Instructions are for one block.

1. Draw a diagonal line on the wrong side of two $2\frac{1}{2}″$ Fabric A squares.

2. Align a marked $2\frac{1}{2}″$ Fabric A square with the left edge of a $2\frac{1}{2}″ \times 4\frac{1}{2}″$ Fabric B rectangle, right sides together, as shown. Sew directly on the marked line and trim, leaving a $\frac{1}{4}″$ seam allowance. Press. Make 4.

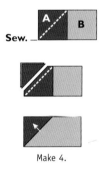

3. Repeat Step 2 to sew a $2\frac{1}{2}″$ Fabric A square to the right edge of each unit. Trim and press. Make 4.

Make 4.

4. Sew a $2\frac{1}{2}″ \times 4\frac{1}{2}″$ Fabric C rectangle to each unit from Step 3 as shown. Press. Make 4.

Make 4.

5. Sew $2\frac{7}{8}″$ Fabric A and $2\frac{7}{8}″$ Fabric B triangles together as shown. Press. Make 8.

Make 8.

6. Sew $2\frac{7}{8}″$ Fabric C and $2\frac{7}{8}″$ Fabric D triangles together as shown. Press. Make 4 units total, 2 using each Fabric D.

Make 2 each (4 total).

7. Arrange and sew 2 units from Step 5, a unit from Step 6, and a $2\frac{1}{2}″$ Fabric B square together as shown. Press. Make 4 units total, 2 using each unit from Step 6.

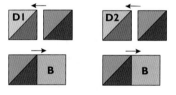

Make 2.   Make 2.

8. Arrange the 4 units from Step 4, the 4 units from Step 7, and a 4½″ Fabric E square as shown. Sew the units and the square together into rows. Press. Sew the rows together. Press.

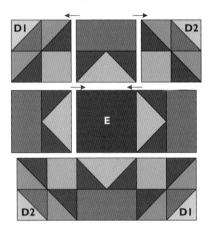

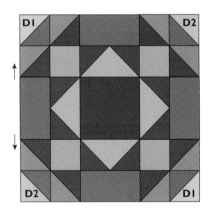

9. Repeat Steps 1–8 to make a total of 9 blocks.

Quilt Assembly

Arrows indicate pressing direction.

1. Refer to the assembly diagram and arrange the blocks in 3 horizontal rows of 3 blocks each.

2. Sew the blocks into rows. Press the seams in opposite directions from row to row.

3. Sew the rows together. Press.

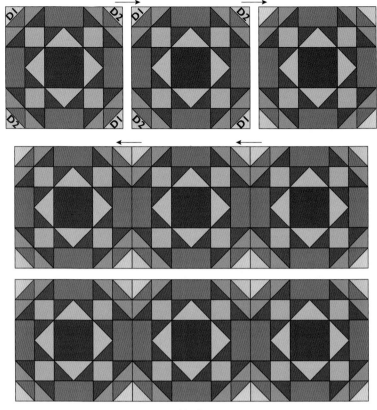

Assembly diagram

4. Sew 3½″ × 48″ outer-border strips to the sides, top, and bottom of the quilt center. Miter the corners and press the seams away from the quilt center.

Finishing Steps

1. If you need help with the finishing process of layering, basting, marking your quilting design, and quilting, refer to your favorite how-to book or to the technical books I have recommended in References (page 94). Otherwise, layer, baste, mark, and quilt in your preferred manner.

2. To prepare the flat mock piping, sew the ³⁄₄″-wide Fabric F strips together end to end with diagonal seams. Press the seams open. Fold the strip in half lengthwise, wrong sides together, and press.

3. Trim the batting and backing even with the raw edge of the quilt top. Measure the quilt through the center from top to bottom and from side to side. Since the quilt is square, these measurements should be the same. Cut 2 strips to each measurement from the long, folded Fabric F strip. With right sides together and raw

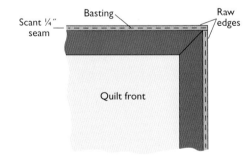

edges aligned, use a machine basting stitch and a scant ¼″ seam allowance to sew the flat mock piping strips to the sides, top, and bottom of the quilt.

4. Bind using your preferred method.

PROJECT 5: Woodland Ocean Waves

The genesis for this quilt was a photographic accident. I was attempting to take a close-up photo of a spider web that was attached to weeds. By the time I had my tripod and camera ready, I had ruined the spider web and caused much of the fluffy part of the weed flower to float away. Disappointed, I looked into my camera's viewfinder anyway and was surprised to see the beautiful, subtle variations of color within the weed seed, the fluff, the stems, and the earth.

I really like this unusual color combination. A fabric selection from this color inspiration is shown on page 91. I chose the Ocean Waves block because it is such a great design for closely related colors.

QUEEN-SIZE BED QUILT

Skill Level: Confident beginner
Number of Blocks: 80
Finished Block Size: 8˝

Woodland Ocean Waves, 74^1/$_2$" × 90^1/$_2$", designed by Joen Wolfrom, pieced by Mickie Swall, machine quilted by Kelly Edwards, bound by Joanne Williams.

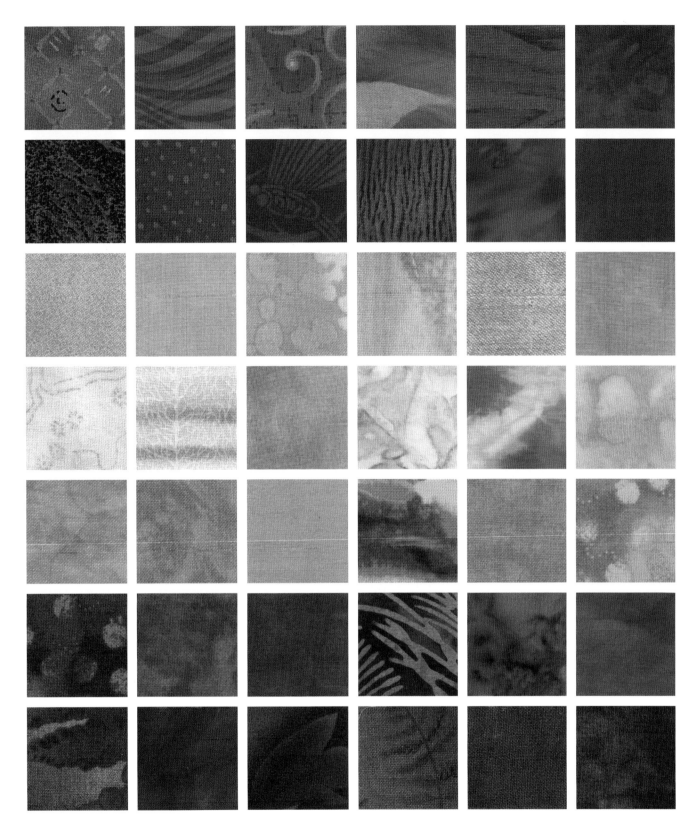

These swatches are a small selection of the dozens of fabrics used in *Woodland Ocean Waves*.

Thoughts About Fabric

As you select your fabrics, be sure to include fabrics with light, medium, and dark values. The colors pulled from the photo are browns; warm rusts; caramel, tan, beige, and taupe; soft, light pinkish-browns; warm greens ranging from light to dark; and a few cool greens.

The Ocean Waves design is created with units of half-square triangles that use value changes and random color placement. You will make triangle units using a combination of light and medium triangles, medium and dark triangles, and light and dark triangles. Mix up the colors, so some units are pairs of greens; some are pairs of browns, rusts, and so on; and some are combinations of the greens and browns (including light pinkish or tan hues). Randomly place these units in the blocks. The large background triangles in the block center should be made from a selection of your lightest warm hues (no greens).

In this quilt, the light fabrics play an effective role in the bands of waves, giving a feeling of the background hues coming through the waves. Since the effect of value is personal, I offer the following suggestion: if you prefer a stronger contrast between your bands of waves and the background, use fewer light fabrics in your bands of waves than you see in this quilt. Simply decrease the number of light half-square triangles used in the small units (don't eliminate them; just replace some with medium and dark fabrics). This change will create a more pronounced contrast to the background. Naturally, if you make this change, you will need to adjust the fabric amounts accordingly. If you are used to using fabrics in a scrappy manner, fabric yardage probably will not be an issue.

FABRIC REQUIREMENTS

Yardages are based on 40"-wide fabric (after washing).

Fabric A: $3^1/8$ yards (total) assorted medium to medium-dark green, rust, and brown subtle or tone-on-tone prints for blocks

Fabric B: $3^1/8$ yards (total) assorted light to light-medium cream, beige, tan, green, pinkish-tan, and taupe subtle or tone-on-tone prints for blocks

Fabric C: $1^1/2$ yards (total) assorted warm (cream, beige, tan, pinkish-brown), light subtle or tone-on-tone prints for blocks*

Outer Border: $2^3/4$ yards medium-dark green tone-on-tone print
Binding: 1 yard
Backing: $5^1/3$ yards (vertical seam)
Batting: 80" × 96" piece
These may be some of the same fabrics you use for Fabric B, but without any light green or taupe prints.

CUTTING

Measurements include $1/4$" seam allowances. Cut strips on the crosswise grain of the fabric (selvage to selvage) unless instructed otherwise.

From Fabric A, cut *a total of*:
- 480 squares, $2^7/8$" × $2^7/8$"; cut once diagonally to make 2 half-square triangles (960 total)

From Fabric B, cut *a total of*:
- 480 squares, $2^7/8$" × $2^7/8$"; cut once diagonally to make 2 half-square triangles (960 total)

From Fabric C, cut *a total of*:
- 80 squares, $4^7/8$" × $4^7/8$"; cut once diagonally to make 2 half-square triangles (160 total)

From the *lengthwise grain* of the outer-border fabric, cut:
- 2 strips, $5^1/2$" × 80"
- 2 strips, $5^1/2$" × 96"

From the binding fabric, cut:
- 9 strips, $3^1/4$" × 40" (double-fold binding sewn with $1/2$" seam; finishes about $1/2$" wide)

OCEAN WAVES BLOCK

You need 80 Ocean Waves blocks for this quilt. Each block is made up of a scrappy mix of Fabric A, Fabric B, and Fabric C. (See Thoughts About Fabric for specific information.)

1. Sew $2^7/8$" Fabric A and $2^7/8$" Fabric B triangles together as shown. Press. Make 800.

Make 800.

2. Sew 3 units from Step 1 together as shown. Press. Make 160.

Make 160.

3. Sew a Fabric A triangle to a unit from Step 2 as shown. Press. Make 80. Sew a Fabric B triangle to each remaining unit from Step 2 as shown. Press. Make 80.

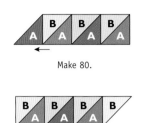

Make 80.

Make 80.

4. Sew 2 remaining units from Step 1 together as shown. Press. Make 160.

Make 160.

5. Sew a Fabric A triangle to a unit from Step 4. Press. Make 80. Sew a Fabric B triangle to each remaining unit from Step 4 as shown. Press. Make 80.

Make 80.   Make 80.

In this quilt, the light fabrics play an effective role in the bands of waves, giving a feeling of the background hues coming through the waves.

6. Arrange and sew 1 of each unit from Step 3 and 1 of each unit from Step 5 together as shown. Press. Sew a Fabric C triangle to the opposite corners as shown. Press. Make 80.

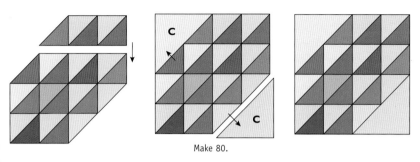

Make 80.

QUILT ASSEMBLY

Arrows indicate pressing direction.

1. Refer to the assembly diagram and arrange the blocks in 10 horizontal rows of 8 blocks each, rotating the blocks as shown.

2. Sew the blocks into rows. Press the seams in opposite directions from row to row.

3. Sew the rows together. Press.

4. Sew 5½″ × 80″ outer-border strips to the top and bottom of the quilt center. Sew 5½″ × 96″ outer-border strips to the sides. Miter the corners and press the seams away from the quilt center.

FINISHING STEPS

If you need help with the finishing process of layering, basting, marking your quilting design, quilting, and binding, refer to your favorite how-to book or to the technical books I have recommended in References (page 94). Otherwise, layer, baste, mark, quilt, and bind in your preferred manner.

Assembly diagram

Suggested References

Technical

All About Quilting From A to Z. Lafayette, CA: C&T Publishing, 2002.

Anderson, Alex. *Finish It with Alex Anderson*. Concord, California: C&T Publishing, 2004.

———. *Start Quilting with Alex Anderson*. 2nd Ed. Concord, California: C&T Publishing, 2001.

Anderson, Alex, Liz Aneloski, Sharyn Craig, Harriet Hargrave. *All-in-One Quilter's Reference Tool*. Concord, California: C&T Publishing, 2004.

Collins, Sally. *The Art of Machine Piecing*. Concord, California: C&T Publishing, 2001.

———. *Borders, Bindings & Edges*. Concord, California: C&T Publishing, 2004.

Craig, Sharyn, Harriet Hargrave. *The Art of Classic Quiltmaking*. Concord, California: C&T Publishing, 2000.

Visual Qualities of a Quilt

Wolfrom, Joen. *Color Play*. Concord, California: C&T Publishing, 2000.

———. *The Magical Effects of Color*. Concord, California: C&T Publishing, 1992.

———. *The Visual Dance*. Concord, California: C&T Publishing, 1995.

Index

About the Author

Joen began quiltmaking in 1974, after she left her career in the education field to become a homemaker and a stay-at-home mom. Her interest in color and design surfaced in the early 1980s. She has taught and lectured in the quilting field, both nationally and internationally, since 1984. Her guest international work has included engagements in England, the Republic of Ireland, Northern Ireland, Scotland, Canada, Germany, Holland, Taiwan, Australia, New Zealand, and South Africa.

In the 1980s, Joen created commissioned textile art for many private clients and corporations. Her work is included in collections throughout the world. Joen is the author of nine books and products. Several have been bestsellers in the arts and crafts field. Her works include *A Garden Party of Quilts, Color Play, Make Any Block Any Size, Patchwork Persuasion, The Visual Dance, The Magical Effects of Color, Landscapes & Illusions, Paper Crafter's Color Companion,* and the *3-in-1 Color Tool.* Joen's earliest bestsellers (*Landscapes & Illusions, The Magical Effects of Color, The Visual Dance*) will be available electronically in 2007.

Joen is the owner of JWD Publishing, a pattern company that publishes designs by leading quiltmakers and designers. These patterns may be purchased at quilt and fabric stores under each designer's pattern-line name.

Joen enjoys working in her garden, reading, photography, hiking, playing bridge, and spending time with her family.

Correspondence may be sent directly to Joen at 104 Bon Bluff, Fox Island, Washington 98333. You may visit Joen's website at www.joenwolfrom.com or her pattern company's website at www.jwdpublishing.com.

Great Titles from

C&T PUBLISHING